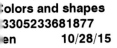

Colors and Shapes

BY KATHY THORNBOROUGH • ILLUSTRATIONS BY KATHLEEN PETELINSEK

The Child's World®

PUBLISHED by The Child's World®
1980 Lookout Drive • Mankato, MN 56003-1705
800-599-READ • www.childsworld.com

ACKNOWLEDGMENTS
The Child's World®: Mary Berendes, Publishing Director
The Design Lab: Design
Jody Jensen Shaffer: Editing

PHOTO CREDITS
© akiyoko/Shutterstock.com: 16; Ballda/Shutterstock.com: 17;
Cherkas/Shutterstock.com: 23; Cloud7Days/Shutterstock.com: 5;
cveltri/iStock.com: 3; D'Vine Photography/Shutterstock.com: cover,
1, 18; homydesign/Shutterstock.com: 19; Ilike/Shutterstock.com:
21; Ivakoleva/Shutterstock.com: 22; Misun/Shutterstock.com: 20;
nednapa/Shutterstock.com: 11; ognianm/iStock.com: 12; Panya
ST/Shutterstock.com: 13; Photo_HamsterMan/Shutterstock.com:
15; Pichi/Shutterstock.com: 10; RapidEye/iStock.com: back cover,
4; rgbdigital/iStock.com: back cover, 9; TaneeStudio/Shutterstock.
com: 14; valzan/Shutterstock.com: 6; Viorika/iStock.com: 8;
weedezign/Shutterstock.com: 7

ISBN 9781626873155
LCCN 2014934485

PRINTED in the United States of America
Mankato, MN
July, 2014
PA02216

A SPECIAL THANKS TO OUR ADVISERS:
*As a member of a deaf family that spans four
generations, Kim Bianco Majeri lives, works,
and plays amongst the deaf community.*

*Carmine L. Vozzolo is an educator of
children who are deaf and hard of hearing,
as well as their families.*

NOTE TO PARENTS AND EDUCATORS:

The understanding of any language begins with the acquisition
of vocabulary, whether the language is spoken or manual. The
books in the Talking Hands series provide readers, both young and
old, with a first introduction to basic American Sign Language
signs. Combining close photocues and simple, but detailed, line
illustrations, children and adults alike can begin the process
of learning American Sign Language. Let these books be an
introduction to the world of American Sign Language. Most
languages have regional dialects and multiple ways of expressing
the same thought. This is also true for sign language. We have
attempted to use the most common version of the signs for the words
in this series. As with any language, the best way to learn is to be
taught in person by a frequent user. It is our hope that this series will
pique your interest in sign language.

Crayons are
made of wax.

Red

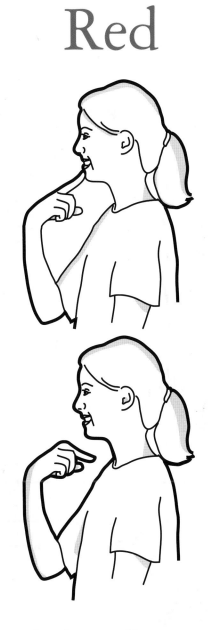

Stroke your lips once
with your finger.

3

Triangle

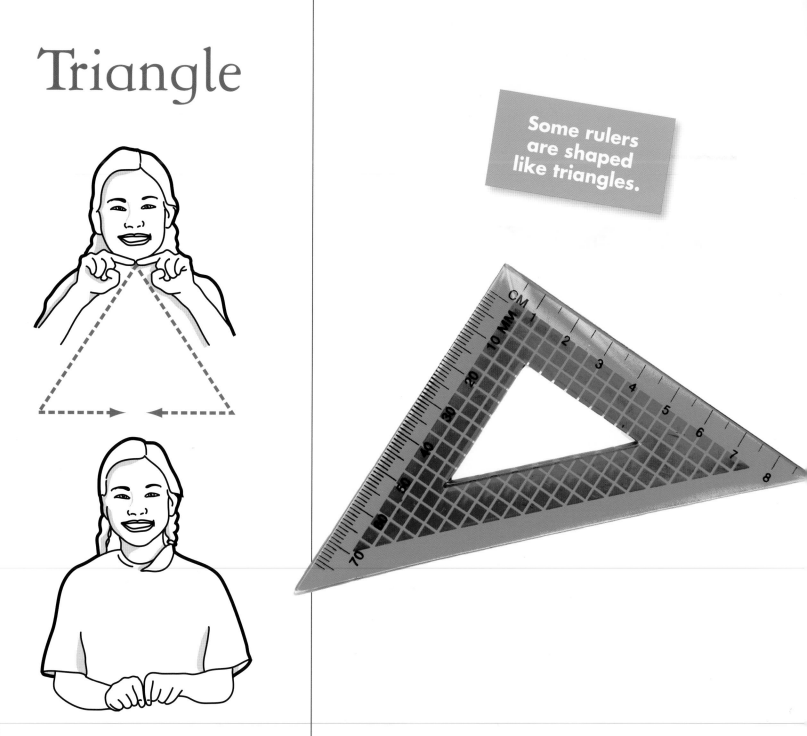

Some rulers are shaped like triangles.

Watermelon

You can eat every part of a watermelon, even the seeds!

Make the "W" sign. Then motion as if you are thumping a melon.

5

Orange

The sign for orange—the color and the fruit—are the same!

Make the "C" sign and then the "S" sign in front of your mouth twice.

6

Circle

A straight line from the center of a circle to the edge is called a radius.

Basketball

Motion as if you are making
an overhead pass twice.

James Naismith
invented
basketball in 1891.

Yellow

Many people think yellow is a cheery color.

Make the "Y" sign. Then twist your wrist a few times.

Rectangle

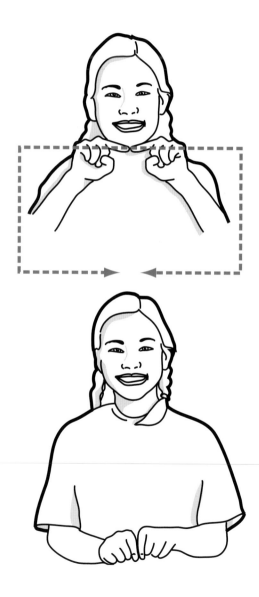

Rectangles have four sides. Two sides are short, and two sides are long.

Cup

Cups with a handle are often used to hold hot drinks.

Make the "C" sign. Tap your flat bottom hand twice.

11

White

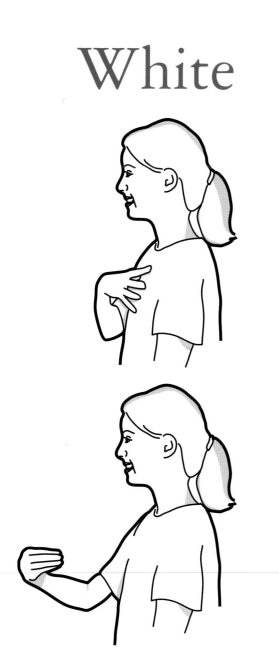

Put a flat hand on your chest.
Pull away and touch your
fingers and thumb.

The color white
sometimes makes
people feel clean
and pure.

Oval

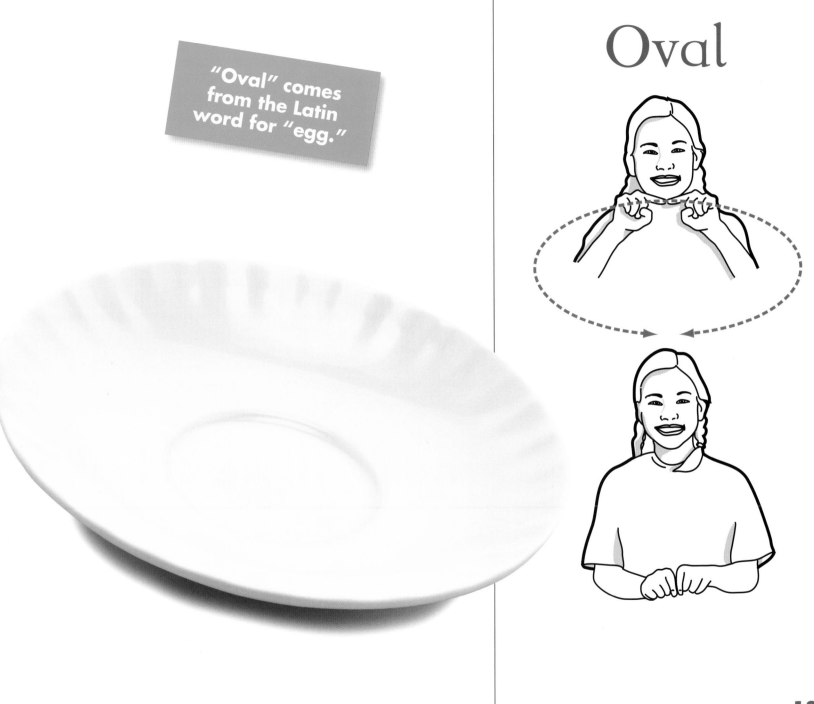

"Oval" comes from the Latin word for "egg."

Egg

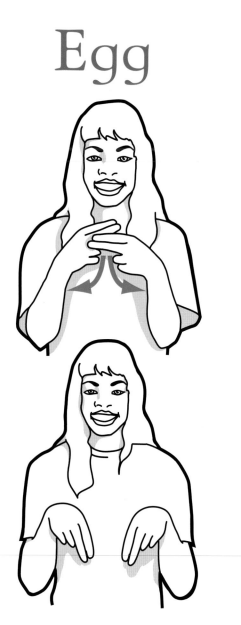

Make the "H" sign with both hands. Tap your fingers together, then move down, as if you are breaking an egg.

The average person eats about 170 eggs a year!

Black

Black is the darkest color.

Move your straight finger from one side of your forehead to the other.

15

Square

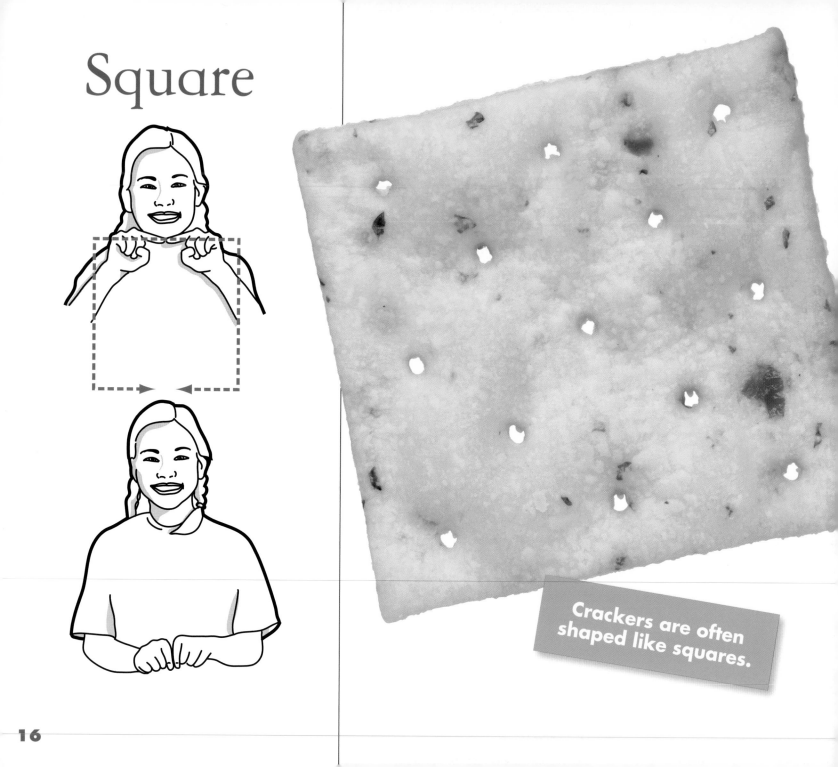

Crackers are often shaped like squares.

Do you have a favorite board game?

Game

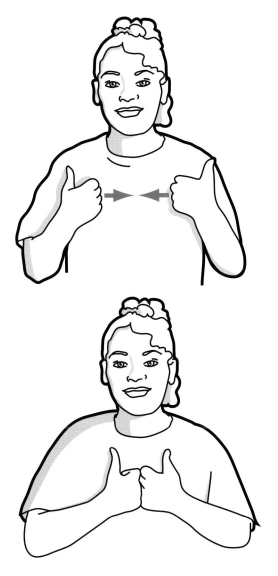

Make the "A" sign with both hands.
Bring them together twice.

Purple

Make the "P" sign. Shake your hand back and forth twice.

Purple starfish like this one live in the Pacific Ocean.

Grapes

Grapes are actually a kind of berry!

Curve one hand. Then make small tapping motions on the back of your other hand.

Blue

Make the "B" sign. Twist your arm at the elbow twice.

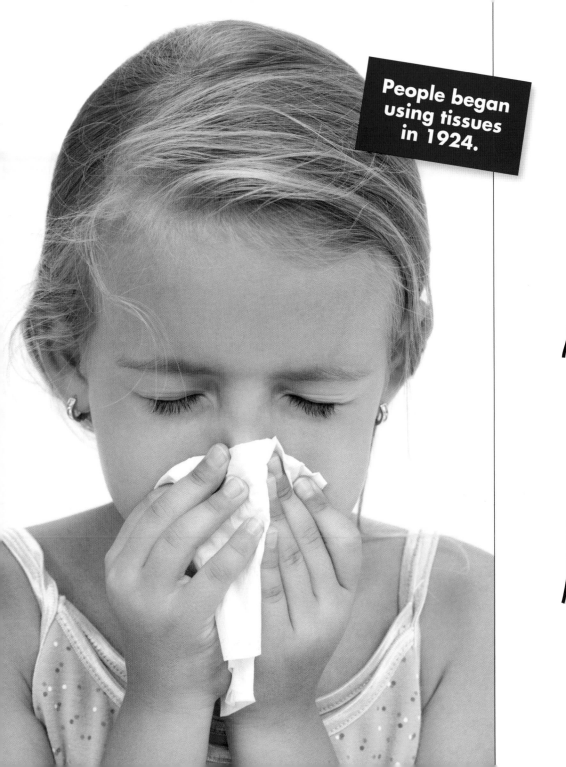

Tissue

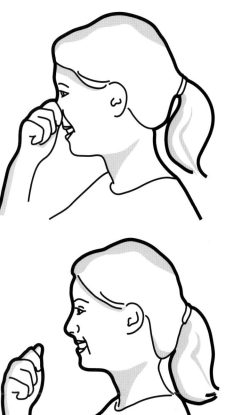

Pretend you are wiping your nose with a tissue.

Green

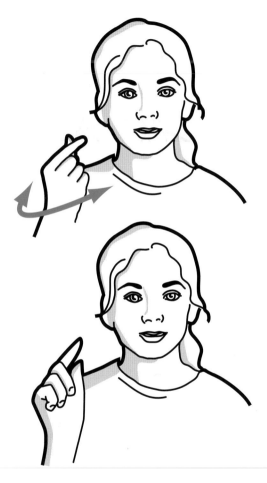

Make the "G" sign. Twist your wrist back and forth

The color green reminds many people of nature.

Bottle

Bottles are often made of glass or plastic.

Make the "C" sign on a flat hand.
Then move up like a bottle.

A SPECIAL THANK YOU!

A special thank you to our models from the Program for Children Who are Deaf and Hard of Hearing at the Alexander Graham Bell Elementary School in Chicago, Illinois.

Aroosa loves reading and playing with her sister Aamna. Aroosa's favorite color is red.

Carla enjoys art, as well as all kinds of sports.

Deandre likes playing football and watching NFL games on television.

Destiny enjoys music and dancing. She especially likes learning new things.

Xiomara loves fashion, clothes, and jewelry. She also enjoys music and dancing.

24